The Practical Guide to Buying HUD Homes

With Real Step-by-Step Instructions

By J. Emerick

© Copyright 2013 J. Emerick

All Rights reserved. No part of this book may be reproduced or transmitted in any form, or by any means, electronic or mechanical, including photocopying and recording, or by any information storage retrieval system without permission in writing from the publisher.

ISBN-10:   1494764504

ISBN-13: 978-1494764500

Contents

Introduction	5
Why Buy HUD Homes?	20
How to Prepare Your Plan	33
The Step-by-Step Process	57
Case Study	72
Resources for Further Study	77

Introduction

My Quest for Financial Security

So you're thinking about buying real estate on the cheap to either rehab and rent, rehab and sell, or perhaps you're looking for a primary residence that is much more affordable than the 'regular' market prices?

Believe me, I've thought about all three options in the last couple of years. In fact, I've been kind of obsessed with real estate and have probably earned the equivalent of Bachelor's degree in the field with all the countless sources of information I've absorbed in just the last fourteen months.

I'm actually a school teacher by trade, and have taught for nearly twenty years in schools all over the country. Now teaching, as you may know, is not a great way to pay the bills. In addition to this, with the current *blame-the-teachers* fad in so-called education *reform*, I personally see no future in education as a career for anyone except overpaid consultants and other 'experts,' but that is not the subject of this book!

Suffice it to say, you wouldn't want your own friends and relatives to be subjected to the daily abuse of vindictive *data-driven* administrators or spoiled *little darlins'* who know you have no power to make them learn - *or behave*! Like many, I think back to choices I made earlier in life, and I see other paths that could have unfolded.

A childhood friend of mine got into computers as a teenager, while I meandered and dabbled in a little of everything. Well, he's making big bucks while I've struggled sometimes to keep my head above water. I'm not bitter about it though. Water under the bridge, I say. If you can't change the past, work on your future!

Well, I've tried many schemes and 'systems' over the years, ever looking for that elusive elixir otherwise known as financial security. I joined multi-level marketing when it started to become hot (anyone remember NuSkin in the 80s?).

I took Tony Robbins courses to learn about 'sales mastery.' I did work for the publishing industry on royalty and I even got into stocks and have invested for over twenty years. Surely, I thought, there must be a way to crack that glass ceiling of wealth! With persistence, I would always start off strong and feel the warm touch of hope in my heart.

Like most people, though, it always seemed that just when you start to get ahead something comes up and you need to call in your resources to take care of one big thing or another. In my case it was buying a primary residence (boom! five years of stock gains sold and invested in a co-op apartment), then having a child to rear (ouch! Another five years of gains called in), and finally, trading up to a house in an expensive part of town (which killed more recent years' efforts worth of investing).

So even though I was always able to make at least *some* money in the market (save for the setback of the recent financial crisis, of course), it never seemed that I could leave that money *alone*.

Tom Reese over at www.dividend.com is very good at encouraging a 'stay-the-course' approach to dividend-paying stocks, and I do follow and appreciate the strategies of both he and the other stock gurus out there – it's just tough when you're not born with a silver spoon in your mouth and you're not in a high flying field that pays you boatloads of money every *month*.

So I looked around, realizing that my meager teaching salary would only modestly rebuild my stock portfolio (and certainly slowly at that), and I tried to envision a way that could truly break me free from this cruel cycle of *get-ahead-and-then-be-pulled-behind* madness.

I had heard about several writers who offered modern advice on how to get ahead for the *regular* guys (and gals), and after some browsing in my local bookstore, I settled on *Rich Dad, Poor Dad* by Robert Kiyosaki. This is one of several books I recommend that you read for yourself.

What did I learn? Mr. Kiyosaki emphasizes a number of things, but one of the main points of argument he hammers home again and again is that real estate is the main vehicle for financial freedom. He mentions stories from his own life to emphasize this fact, and he uses the backdrop of his *poor dad* to illustrate the dangers of thinking small.

His *rich dad* was all about thinking big and conceiving of plans on a grand, imaginative scale. This sounded like great advice to me, but what was missing from this book was the nuts-and-bolts of real estate.

I realized quickly that Mr. Kiyosaki's purpose was more esoteric in nature. He wanted to convince you of the need to change your thinking about what was *possible*. If you wanted the nitty-gritty, you had to widen your dragnet and pull in more experts.

You would need to learn from people who would show you the ropes. There would be books to read, seminars to attend, people to talk to – wait a minute – isn't all of that what keeps people from getting started to begin with?!

I had to find another way – one that was a better use of my time. I settled on whatever I could learn on the internet. This actually is a great way to learn anything. The internet is full of free information. In my school the other teachers rave about Khan Academy, Youtube videos and other free teaching websites.

Here I would find some virtual experts to model. Indeed, one of the things I will always remember from my Tony Robbins seminars was his insistence on 'modeling success.' So I set out from *Rich Dad, Poor Dad* to find internet-based real estate experts I could model.

Before I go further, keep in mind that my foray into real estate investing has been very recent. My primary residences were never, in my mind, *investments*. This is the place I live, and as any married person will tell you, it's not entirely *mine* either, so I was literally starting from scratch with this.

Where do I learn? What internet sources can I trust? Do I have to spend a lot of money to make a lot of money first? These were questions that daunted me in the beginning. I am sure you also have wondered about this: where do I find out how to do *it* – how to invest in and profit from real estate? It was in these early stages that I resolved to constantly remember my primary motivation: the desire to one day be freed from a job that is getting increasingly difficult for all teachers.

So newly armed with the mantra to *take action*, I searched around for those whom I could model. My first choice was teaching videos on Youtube. Type in 'real estate investing' and you will get tons of great links.

Watch a few – they're usually never very long and you can learn a lot of important things that help you understand what you need to learn after that. Quick, painless and fits in with your schedule - what a great concept in education!

Now like most people with an email account, I am perpetually bombarded with junk mail and spam. Some of those include subject headings that are related to money, getting rich quick and related matters.

One day I got an email from Bryan Ellis – of course it was an email sent to hundreds of thousands of others, but the subject line read 'real estate investing,' so I opened it and read it. It offered to subscribe me to a free real estate investing newsletter, so on a whim I went to the website and plugged in my email.

Mr. Ellis has a great newsletter, and what I like about him is his honesty and broad interest in things even beyond real estate. [1] Subscribing to such newsletters is free, so I recommend getting all the free advice you can get!

Now I don't know if these guys in the often labeled 'guru industry' sell each other their mailing lists, but soon I was the recipient of other *offers of insight and guidance* from

---

[1] www.investing.bryanellis.com is the address for his website.

other real estate masters. There was Jack Bosch, Rob Swanson, John Cochran and most recently, Dustin Hahn. All of them offered programs to buy that promised to make you real estate moguls in a pinch.

After having tried a few other get-rich-quick schemes in the past, I knew it was never so easy as an expert says. It is *easy* for the expert, but that's because they're the *expert*!

They had a tremendous amount of drive (and possibly good luck or fortunate circumstances) that propelled them into the stratosphere of their fields. For regular people like you and me, it isn't always easy to just *go for it* like that. Work, family, other current obligations and even self-doubts (or just plain laziness) often keep us from getting *anything* new started.

It is true that change doesn't come without pressure or tragedy. Thank God tragedy was never needed to get me motivated, but being sick and tired of living paycheck to paycheck, and seeing a future as an old man living a hard, deprived life, finally goaded me into trying to get myself 'set up' for a worry-free *now* and a comfortable *future* (now that's pressure).

I know how hard it is to get started on something new, and real estate must seem especially daunting – that's why I am writing this book – to show how you can get started without really upsetting your life too much. There is a way to get the ball rolling, and the main ingredient is to show you step-by-step how to do the actual process.

I say 'actual process' because this is what I wanted from the real estate gurus I mentioned before. They all had something to sell, namely, their 'systems' for doing real estate. I don't begrudge them for that – hey, they're opening up another income stream and sharing their advice to those who want it. I was just really hesitant to spend a lot of money on something that might not work for me.

I also couldn't see myself going to tax lien auctions all over the place, buying raw land in places thousands of miles away, setting up computer matrix-like systems where I 'wholesale' houses by the dozens every month, spending hours on the phone making deals with other peoples' money, cold calling mourning relatives to buy their loved ones' houses and so forth.

Hey, *I still gotta make my lesson plans for class tomorrow*, and I don't want to mess up my pension prospects – which is one of the greatest sources of future income streaming still existing in the world today!

So what did I do? I listened to all their webinars, which were free, and I saw that these men knew what they were talking about. Strangely enough, by combining together the free information they individually used as teasers, I was able to develop strategies that served as a launching pad to building my own real estate empire.

I did also download a lot of ebooks about real estate investing, but I (half) read only one, and it wasn't helpful – besides, there's little time to read in my busy life. From the skimming I did on some of the others, the same problem was present – these writers mostly talk of a grand scale of investing that requires more work than I (and many other people) can give right now.

Which strategy should I choose to start? What would work best on a 'small scale' to at least get me started? These questions occupied my thoughts for some time.

So after weighing many different approaches, I decided to zero in on one real estate investing strategy that I had heard about over the years, but never knew how to do: buying HUD homes! Each of the real estate gurus are experts in their own rights, and I believe their systems are sound and honest in their aims.

I also respect them for their energy and forthrightness. I wouldn't mind hanging out with any of them! I just feel that for my scale and circumstance, one simple, low commitment strategy will work best.

I don't know what your ambitions are – whether you want to buy HUD homes on a fast and vast scale, or if you are like me, wanting to pick up a few per year and rent them out eventually being ready to retire with peace of mind. Whichever road you choose, the path as I lay it out before you will serve both aims.

This particular book, in fact, is an account of my efforts to start my own real estate empire in my quest for financial freedom. Unlike many other books on the market, I spend little time theorizing and cajoling to action, and instead focus on the nuts and bolts of how to do a deal and get a HUD house for cheap.

It's because I couldn't find this approach explained so clearly in other venues that I felt strongly about sharing my experience going through the process with others. Over the course of the last couple of months, when I shared this knowledge with my colleagues (fellow teachers) and revealed details about deals I was making, they were dumbfounded and wanted me to show *them* how to do it themselves.

In fact, this very day, the catalyst for coming home from work and writing this book came from our school's math teacher who said, "I want to sit down with you so you can show me how to do it." I spent about twenty minutes showing him the exact process I used to get $20,000 to $40,000 homes for between $3000 and $7000 dollars.

When I was finished, (and the buzzer rang, signaling it was time for the next class to begin,) he looked at me and said, "You've given me ideas." Later on, as he passed me in the hall, he looked at me right in the face and repeated the exact phrase again.

Now I want to give *you* ideas, because this HUD buying program is the best thing I have EVER seen for realistic financial security and long term wealth building for the future. I will be walking you through the deal from start to finish, leaving nothing out, and I will illustrate this with two actual houses that I closed on this same month.

My hope is that you, too, can get started towards your path of economic improvement, and if I only help one person get a great deal that can change their life for the better, then I feel I have done my job. Read on, fair one, and prosper in your own real estate empire!

Why Buy HUD Homes?

About six years ago I looked at my life and realized I had no real assets other than my share of the house I lived in with my family. I knew people who had real estate investments, and one of my wife's cousins was a real estate agent, so dinner parties usually included some elements of this or that person talking about one high flying deal or another.

I eagerly participated in these discussions, but I knew I was just another wallflower here: always a bridesmaid and never a bride, so to speak.

I wished I could buy and sell houses too, like the high rollers in and around my life. I remember how flummoxed I was when I learned that a peripheral figure in my school (of the time) owned not one, but two whole apartment buildings – and 18 houses to boot! I really wanted in on some of that! I briefly thought about becoming a real estate agent, but then I realized that I had no interest in showing strangers other peoples' houses all day long.

Whatever I did, I wanted to do on my own. Of course, having little money didn't actually help me. Sure I was putting money in stocks as I could, but that was growing slower than I needed, and life changes forced me to drain my accounts not once, but three times over the subsequent years. Clearly, the stock market wasn't going to help here.

So a little while after that time I started to look more closely at some of the real estate websites that we dabbled with in my household – that is, when we dreamt of buying a bigger or better house somewhere *else*. The first website was www.trulia.com. This is a great website that is definitely user friendly and even fun to use.

If you have even a passing interest in real estate, I encourage you to play around with this and other similar websites so you can begin to get a 'feel' for an area and get generally familiar with housing prices by region, city and town.

You don't have to create an account to use it, but if you do, the website allows you to 'save' properties that you're interested in remembering. The website will also email you 'suggestions' from time to time, based on your saved searches.

I like the interactive maps that show comparable prices around the house you may be looking at, as well as local crime statistics, schools and other factors that may raise or lower the esteem of the house in question that you're considering.

Later on I also found out about www.zillow.com. This is another website that is very popular, and it serves the same basic function as Trulia. I strongly prefer the Trulia interface, as the Zillow one can seem bulky and unwieldy. (It used to be better, but of late they keep tweaking it and trying to make it look more trendy and full of big splashy sections.) The Zillow site does have different resources listed for each home, though, so it is still worth a look.

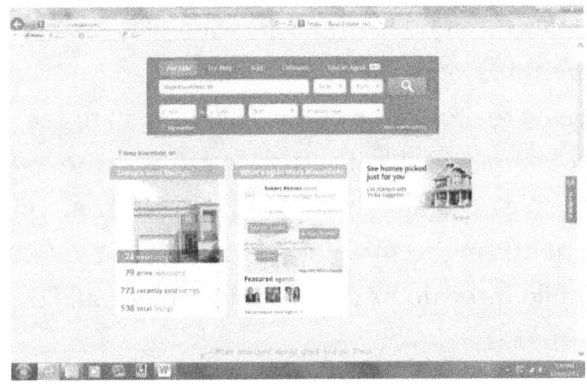

Now one thing you may notice between these two websites is that Trulia tends to low ball the house prices, while Zillow tends to overestimate them. Case in point: I bought a HUD home in Ecorse, MI that Trulia said was worth $19,000, while Zillow said it was worth $43,000! What a spread that is!

As they say, only by contacting a local real estate agent for an appraisal will get you the most accurate prices. What I've found though is that the 'true' price can often be gleaned by just meeting the Trulia and Zillow prices in the middle. It's a rough estimate, but I, personally, have found it to be close to accurate.

As I continued my exploration of these two websites, and a few others like www.realtor.com and the like, I began to see some really wildly fluctuating prices in the Michigan county that I always focused on. On one street you may have a house for $125,000 while three doors down another one could by $49,000.

Why the discrepancy? Ah, it was foreclosures – bank foreclosures, specifically. The foreclosed houses were really worth more that what you saw, but the bank just wanted to get rid of the properties fast. [2]

Of course, as you know, this glut of foreclosures really distorted a lot of markets. As of this writing real estate analysts talk of a strengthening of the housing market overall. Of course there is the 'shadow inventory' of off-market foreclosed homes that is still waiting in the wings, but whether or not another glut occurs, real estate is always

---

[2] Sadly, www.auction.com listings also have begun appearing on Trulia, and this is muddying the picture a little.

better for weathering the storms than the stock market. [3]

I looked upon these bank foreclosures longingly. I could get a $100,000 house for half that! What a deal! Trouble is, I didn't have "half that." I resolved to keep my eyes open and try to save up some money, if I could, though I knew it was a long shot. [4]

After the financial crisis of '07-'08 was righting itself, my stock investments began to pick up steam. I was actually surprised that a few thousand dollars, deposited and invested over just about three years ('09-'11) suddenly grew as some of my individual stocks took off.

By July of 2012, I was feeling very confident (success, however mild, tends to do that). I still didn't have enough to pay for a

---

[3] I am not advocating abandoning the stock market, even though I might make jabs here and there. I believe in a balanced portfolio of investments including real estate, stocks, precious metals and other similar things.

[4] There is an entire industry of gurus who advocate buying bank foreclosures. Signing up for www.realtytrac.com is a good place to start if you want to keep abreast of the deals.

foreclosure, but at least I felt better about myself. I decided to keep my eyes open a little more.

On a fluke, while on summer vacation in Michigan, I happened to see a sign in a real estate agency's window. It said, "**Free Foreclosure List**." I don't know why, but I turned my car around and pulled into the parking lot. I went inside and asked for a flier from the lovely lady at the front desk. I took the list home and realized the prices were actually not half bad.

I still was shy at least five thousand dollars to even touch the cheapest one, but I felt oh, so *close*. I went back to that real estate office and asked for an agent to show me around some properties that I was interested in. This is one of the most important things you can do, as a real estate investor: build a relationship with a real estate agent.

They are more than happy to show you around, and they are even happier to make a sale, but they understand this business – they will have a lot of clients who ultimately won't buy, at least right away, so they are looking ahead, hoping that when you are ready to buy, that you will remember them and return to them.

The agent and I drove around the sleepy little town in Michigan where I wanted to invest and he showed my several houses over the course of about a week. I found one I really, really liked and discussed with him my options.

It wasn't a bank foreclosure but it was still really cheap at $50,000. I sheepishly offered $39,000 and to my surprise, the offer was accepted the next day. I didn't think it would go through, so I scrambled around for a source of funding.

At the time I had only about $28,000 (saved over many years of scrimping, saving and investing). [5] I figured I would get a mortgage for the rest, then put a renter in it

---

[5] I know for many people, $28k may seem like a big chunk of change to have, and they may say, "Well, I can only muster a fraction of that." I agree, and normally that was my case, but as we shall see, you will only need a small amount of money to get into HUD homes. Bank foreclosures are a much higher market for sure.

to pay the expenses. It seemed like a good deal because the house was worth probably about $65,000 and it needed no rehab at all.

Here is the actual Property Below:

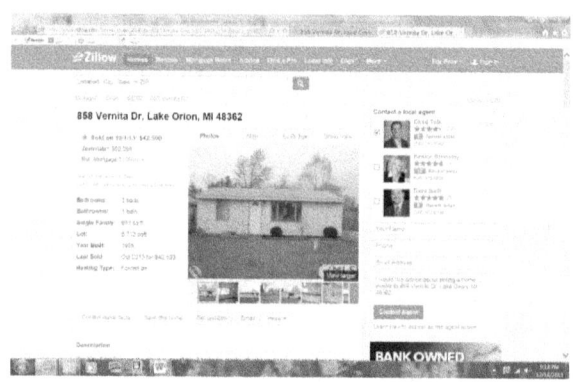

To my surprise, I couldn't get a loan for such a small amount. It turns out that banks won't lend for houses if the loan is under $50,000 grand. My real estate agent knew a guy who specialized in smaller loans, but that didn't pan out either. Then I realized that the market for bank foreclosed houses under $50,000 is dominated by cash buyers. Sadly, I felt defeated. Little did I realize my fortunes would turn.

By the end of July my vacation was over and I retreated back to the East Coast to commiserate and prepare for my impending doom – er, I mean return to work! Then it happened, one of my stocks was being bought out by another company. (It happens from time to time and when it does, you could get really lucky!)

Suddenly, I have $5,000 extra. The previous home was still out of reach, but another bank foreclosure I had seen was possible – in fact, the price had dropped a whopping 10k just the day before (now it was 39k). The bank really wanted to get rid of it!

I got on the phone and asked the real estate agent to put a bid on it for $33,000. Amazingly it was accepted! I scraped the last couple thousand together and bought my first investment property for $34,000 (there was one thousand in closing costs). I felt like I was on top of the world – your first property will have that affect on you! Of course, I didn't think much about the rehab process – or its costs – and that actually turned out to be more than I expected.

Rehabbing a foreclosed home, which is usually necessary, is a bit of a learning curve for investors, and I was no different. Cost overruns and delays gave me a sour taste in my mouth. I wound up spending over $20,000 over the course of the next 14 months (most of it borrowed – yikes!) and I quickly saw it was an untenable business model. Even after I installed a renter in that house, I realized, it will still take me years to recoup those monies! Clearly, there had to be a better way.

This is where the real estate gurus came in handy. They all had different programs and schemes ranging from tax deed/lien sales to wholesale 'flipping.' I took a mental catalog of each 'system' and zeroed in on one that I liked. Indeed, one of the most interesting webinars I saw from one of them was about HUD homes. Like I mentioned previously, I had heard about them, but never really understood how they worked. I even remember hearing wild stories about "Homes for $1" and other such teasers.

Well, this webinar, which revealed only just enough to make you want to buy the guru's 'system' for $997 or some number like that, piqued my interest. I certainly wasn't going to buy his system, because I knew the information was free out there on the internet if I was willing to look for it, (and I was). In fact, it became crystal clear to me that, as a regular guy with only limited funds, buying bank foreclosed or low end market-rate houses, even if they were lower than regular price, was a non-starter.

Truly, regular bank foreclosed homes were out of my league. Yeah, sure - the house may be 50% lower than it should be due to the bank discount, but that was still many tens of thousands more than I could afford, and I was still reeling from my first experience, what with all the rookie mistakes I made in the rehab process.

Anyway, so I went to the website that the guru in question talked about: www.hudhomestore.com. This is the website the government uses to dispose of the homes that it took possession of due to foreclosure from its own lending arms (Freddie Mac, Fannie Mae, etc), or other means.

Once there, I played around with it and almost immediately I saw the possibilities. Are there homes on this website for $100,000 or more? Yes, but there's also homes for $1,000, $3,000 and $5,000 too. Just perfect to get your feet wet and snap up some cheap rentals or fix and flips.

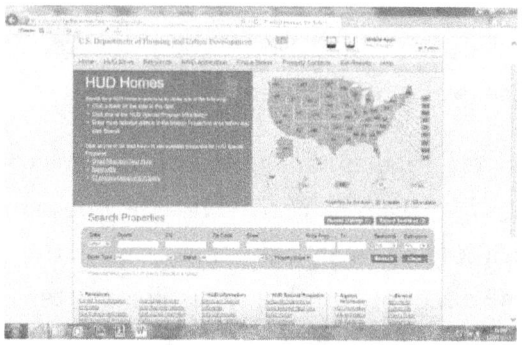

So at this point, I've set aside any notion of regular bank foreclosed properties. Sure, they're good deals in principle, but for the beginning real estate investor with limited means, or the seasoned investor who is looking for quantity, HUD homes are the way to go.

As you will see in the coming chapters, it is a lot easier to buy a HUD home than you think!

How to Prepare Your Plan

There are several elements of planning that can make smooth your entry into HUD home buying. Of course, this advice would work equally well if you plan on going after bank foreclosures or more traditional market-rate properties.

This advice is culled from a variety of sources that I personally viewed, read, conversed with or watched. Indeed, I've tested a lot of techniques and 'systems' until I found what works for the entry level investor. Why do I say *entry level investor*? Because that was *me* and this book is the chronicle of how I broke into this field.

I'm not a guru, nor do I plan to set up websites, package 'systems,' do mass e-mailing, create computer programs or give seminars. I'm just a regular guy who wants to buy a few houses every year as cheaply as possible to fix and rent out for extra income for today and tomorrow.

So I probably should mention here that any of the techniques or advice I give are strictly non-professional and that I cannot be held liable for what people do or do not do with it. (All the gurus give this disclaimer, so I will 'model' them on this too!)

Okay, back to the planning. This part does not require any investment in money, and you don't need to spend a lot of time either. This was one of the things that made me not sign on to the guru systems out there. I wanted to buy houses, but I didn't want to devote hours and hours every week to it.

In a nutshell, your planning consists of four main areas. These are:

1) Knowing the Terrain: In other words, getting educated about the specific area in which you want to invest – which includes reaching out to a real estate agent and getting to know him or her

2) Website Research: This is where you learning how to use the relevant websites that will keep you on top of the game and give you leads and actionable intelligence
3) Fix'er Up: Learning how to calculate and plan for rehabs
4) Paying the Bill: Knowing how to get your money together and how to get it where it needs to go on time

So let's take these four elements and explore them.

Knowing the Terrain

This part of the planning requires you to do the following things:

Decide where you want to invest in homes

Learn how to use Trulia, Zillow, City-Data and the Hud Home Store websites

Identifying a real estate agent you can work with and making contact and building the relationship

How do you decide where to invest? For me it was easy. I love the county in Michigan where I grew up. Even though I no longer live there, I know the place and have a good idea about the various towns and values.

Perhaps you also want to invest close to home, or close to a previous place you called home, or maybe you have set your eyes on a state far away.

I considered doing that too. I've long heard that Texas, Colorado and Arizona are great places to invest. A work colleague of mine has seven rental properties down in Florida and swears by it.

I personally advise to let your first deal or two be closer to home. Why, you ask? Because you can travel to the area, stop in to real estate agents' offices and make contact with real live people. There's no substitute for firsthand knowledge, especially if you plan to sink money in an area.

The real estate agent you feel comfortable working with can show you houses and give you a feel for how the process works and how to judge houses. It's FREE education folks. I deem this essential.

You should also make sure, and this is very important, that the final agent you decide to work with is registered to place bids on the Hud Home Store website.

The HUD Homestore Website

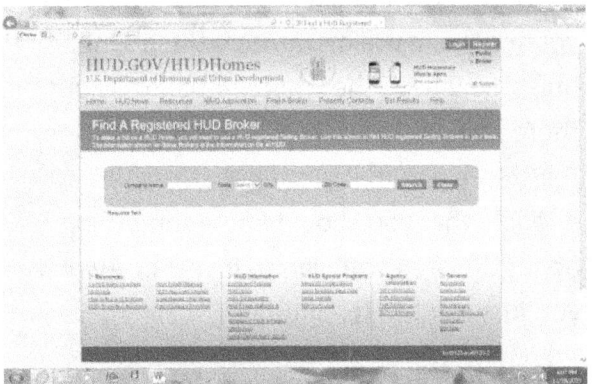

How do you find that out? Well, you can ask them, or you can preselect an agent or agency in advance.

Go to www.hudhomestore.com and click on the "Find a Broker" link under the main banner. A menu will open up and you can search by state. (The state is all that is required to specify.) When the list comes up, there's your list. Not every real estate agent is registered – in fact most aren't, so to save some time this is best to do in advance. You can still work with other agents to educate you, but you will need that registered broker.[6]

If you are insistent on making deals far away on the other side of the country, well, your contacts will be through the phone, unless you have the wherewithal to fly out there and get to know the area and the local registered agent(s). I cannot stress this enough, that you should know something about the area you plan to invest in, even if you just want to fix-and-flip.

I have read horror stories of people who bought homes they thought were great deals, but it turns out the homes were in dangerous

---

[6] It is always recommended that you inspect a HUD home personally before you buy, or at least have a real estate person take a look. After that, a home inspection is allowed within a certain timeframe. You will find, however, that these options are impractical either due to distance, cost or the need for speed. More about this later.

ghetto areas, and they couldn't even give the houses away and wound up losing money. [7]

Website Research

Okay, so let's assume you identified an area you want to buy in, and you made contact with a real estate agent, who is also Hud registered and willing to show you around (in-person or through virtual means like video). What's next?

This is where you and your computer will get to know each other better. Now the real estate gurus promote their computer-based 'systems' to buy and sell homes with a passion, and I have no doubt that they are completely workable. I must reiterate that for regular folks like me, who don't want to be real estate moguls, such 'systems' are – in a word -overkill.

---

[7] It is not always wrong to invest in blighted areas. Sometimes you can buy tremendous house value, and rent them out to Section 8 tenants who don't mind living in the area because they're used to it. I personally recommend buying in the suburban areas just outside the blighted zones. Rents are higher and the deals are still there without all the risk.

I just want to buy a few houses a year for personal income security. I'm generally happy with my life as is and don't want to travel the world in a yacht or spend months in Tahiti.

So rather than something on the order of complex 'systems,' I will lay out some great do-it-yourself internet research techniques that will arm you with all you need to do this in a painless and easy way. Here is a run-down of how I do my basic research to know more about an area, comparable home values and potential gains and losses in a general sense.

www.Trulia.com

This is a great website for beginners. It has an intuitive interface and gives good general information and some detailed facts, as well. Type in a city and state, or a zip code to get all the active listings in an area.

You can, of course, narrow down the parameters by price, number of bedrooms, and so forth. You really need to play with this website and check it often to really get a 'feel' for the market in an area. I personally spend about ten minutes on Trulia about four to five times a week.

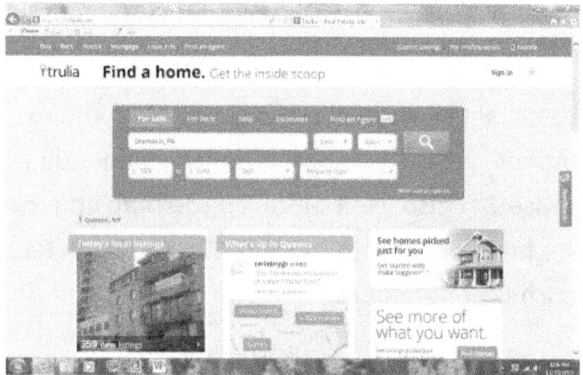

You can also check local rents, get estimates, find an agent and many other things you may find of use. [8] At the bottom of the webpage they have hotlinks to major foreclosure markets and also rental hubs.

The main thing you want to do on Trulia is use it to find out more about the HUD homes you are interested in, along with comparables and the surrounding area. When you find a

---

[8] Trulia has a nice foreclosure buying education center. www.trulia.com/guides/foreclosure. Of course, it is very general, not step-by-step, and relies heavily on the bank foreclosure as its subject matter, but for general tips and pointers it's pretty good.

home on the HUD Homestore website, just copy and paste the address into Trulia to get more information on the home.

You can scroll down the page to see the financial history of the house, historic values and look at the comparables [9] to surrounding houses.   I also like to look on the map and use the tabs for "crimes," "schools," and such to learn more about the area.

Let's say you put in a search for houses in general in an area on the Trulia main page. Let's say, "Reno, NV." When the list of homes comes up, there's two neat things to do.

First, choose the "Map" tab option at the top of the list of homes. Then when the map pops up, tick off the box on the far right side of the webpage that says, "Search within the Map."

This allows you to move the map around (by grabbing it with your mouse) and seeing

---

[9] "Comparables" means to look at the prices of houses nearby that are of similar size and age to get an approximate idea of what your potential house is really worth.

homes for sale in surrounding areas outside that city or zip code. You can also (from the "List" tab option) filter the results from "Lo-Hi" which can reveal many foreclosed homes at the top of your list. HUD homes are sometimes listed on this and other websites.[10]

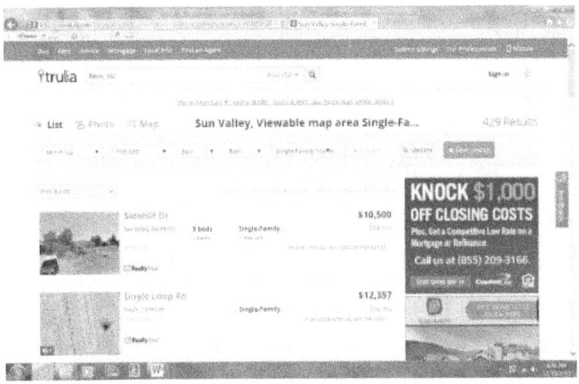

So Trulia is good to get an idea about a local market, to understand price ranges, to know about average local rents an also to know about pertinent statistics that could affect the value and success of your home buying foray (such as local crime, etc). Trulia

---

[10] Beware the listings that appear on Trulia from auction.com. You have to go over to auction.com to bid on those, and the requirements to get the ball rolling are onerous.

also has a built-in blog where people discuss local conditions.

Remember, you're not devoting your life to this or any other website. You're just using it as a reference from time-to-time and, depending on your zeal, you may use it a lot or a little and still get good information you can use.

www.Zillow.com

Zillow is similar to Trulia. The interface is a little more unwieldy, but it also is a good source of information. There are similar tools, and when I'm interested in a particular HUD house, I put the address in both websites to see what each has to say about it.

As I mentioned previously, both websites give different estimates of value. Trulia undervalues homes, while Zillow overvalues them. The trick is to average the price between the two.

Another feature I like on Zillow is the price history it gives for each house. You can see historical house data going back about ten years on your prospective home. It also often has links to county websites. See the screenshot from Zillow below.

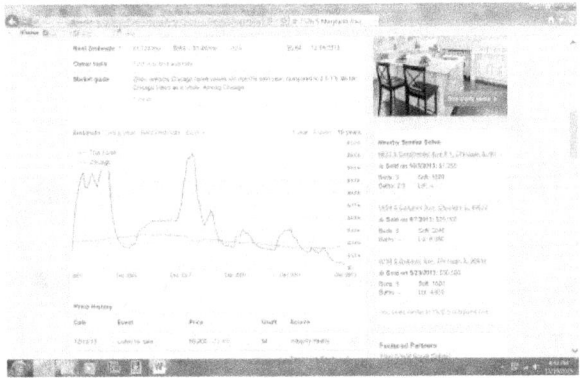

www.City-Data.com

Let's say you found a home on the HUD Homestore and you've looked it up on both Trulia and Zillow (and possibly realty.com or realtor.com), and you are really, really interested in it. Is that all the research you need to do? Not quite.

You still need more demographic and other relevant data before you call the real estate agent and say, "Bid, bid bid!" This is where a boring statistics website comes in. City-data.com is great for filling in the rest of the story on that house.

City-data collects census information, local economic conditions and other goodies of all kinds to tell you exactly what's going on in that geographic location.

A Screenshot of the City-Data Main Page

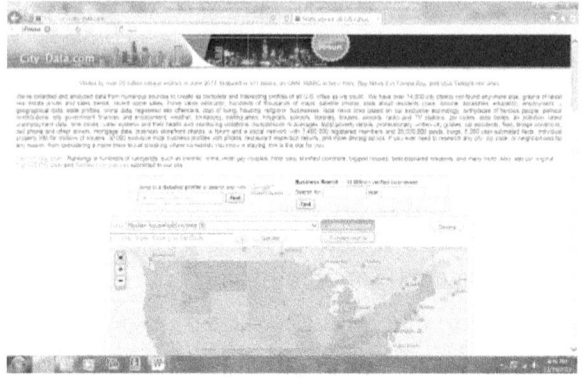

From the main screen, go to the box that says, "Jump to a detailed profile" and type in a zip code. Hit enter, and then you will be amazed at the data that comes up. Medium income, demographics, percent of renter vs homeowners, education levels – it goes on and on and on.

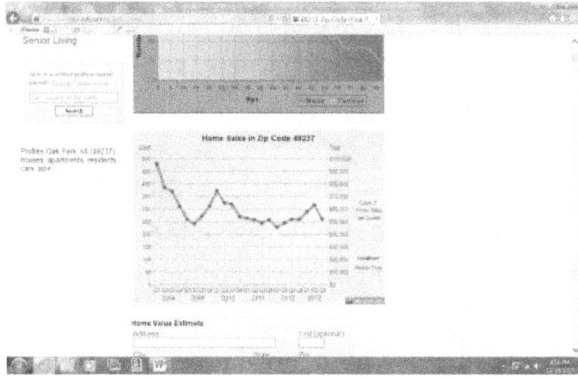

Now you don't need to get too cerebral here. You don't need to study or memorize the information either. Depending on your level of fastidiousness you will either take a quick glance at a few factors or really get to know how well your future investment might do.

Personally, I look at only six main statistics when considering if I want to buy a HUD home in that area. They are:

1) Demographics
2) Renters vs Homeowners
3) Education Level
4) Home Sales in the Zip Code
5) Income levels
6) Local industries

You will soon develop your own favorite stats to determine if a particular home and area is good for your own investment interest.

I highly recommend that you check this website every time you consider buying a HUD home (or any other home for that matter).

www.hudhomevalue.com

This is a nice little website, especially if you like to see what the final bids were on recently sold Hud homes. It also lists current homes for sale.

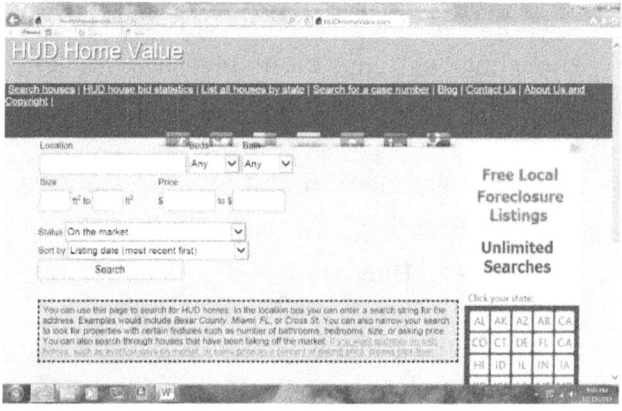

You can search by state and get the final "Bid Result" so you can see how far the original price HUD offered is from the final bid they accepted.

Below and on the next page you will see screen shots of this useful information.

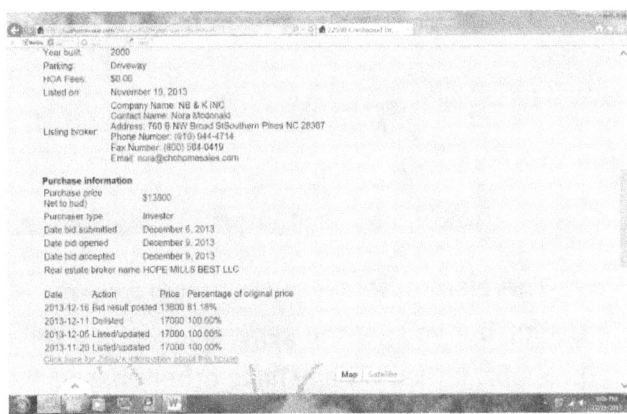

Look at the bottom section where it says "Date" and "Action". This is where you see the action as it played out. You can also check the house you are interested in on this website.

If it is still active on the HUD Homestore, you might see some price history here. This is especially useful just in case some other bidder won the listing, but then could not follow through and the home was relisted, possibly at a lower price.

Look how many times this house fell through

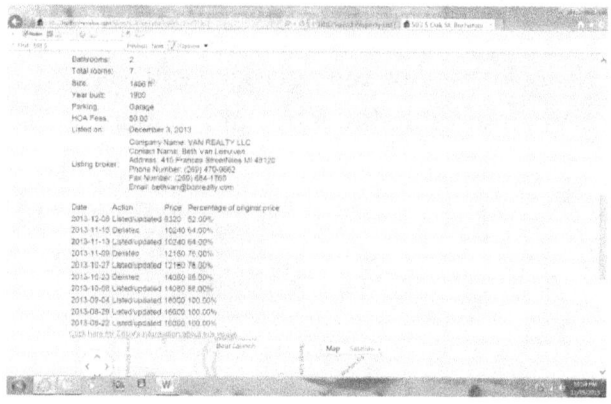

There are other websites that are also useful, but you get the general idea. You will probably either already have other ones in mind, or you will come to add them to your stable of resources as you come across them.

The point is to do this background investigative work to fully understand if any particular house is worth your time. I followed this method and won two great HUD homes in the space of three weeks of each other. I am still pinching myself about that. I almost feel like I'm stealing those houses because the deals were just too good. But I did my internet homework and swooped in on deals that may have been overlooked by other investors.

Of course, the one website we have not talked about yet is the actual HUD Homestore website. We'll go into that one in the next chapter when we go through an exercise in how to buy homes from that site.

Fix'er Up

Okay. These are HUD homes we're looking at here. (Bank foreclosures may also fit into this discussion too.) We're not generally talking move-in condition.

People lost these homes. People possibly abused these homes, or didn't keep them up. Vandals may have invaded these homes. Time or the elements may have caused some damage.

If you're looking at the higher end HUD homes, perhaps you will see gem after gem that needs no more than a for sale sign on the front lawn.

If you're like me, looking for the lower-priced bargains, you will have some rehab work in your future. These costs must be calculated into your overall budget and potential profit margins.

It is often hard to know what's wrong with a house unless you have it inspected. It is possible to have a HUD home inspected, especially if you buy one on a loan.

There's usually about a ten day window to have the inspection done in which time you can still cancel the contract.

If you're buying on cash the inspections get more tricky because HUD wants to rush you to the close so quickly. Your real estate agent needs to be on your same wavelength about this and must be willing to help make this a reality. You will have to pay for the inspection, of course, and it can be several hundred dollars.

If you're buying long-distance, there will be times when it is not practical for a home inspection. Hey, it happens sometimes. In those instances you have to ballpark the condition of the house as much as possible.

Three options lay open before you if you can't get the house inspected.

1) Look for Trulia and Zillow photos. They might have more than the HUD listing. If you see on those websites the name of the listing agent, [11] you might be able to go to their website directly to see if there's more pictures.

2) You can see what HUD has to say about the house. Did you know they inspect the houses before they put them up for sale? They also winterize them too!

   When you click on a HUD home listing on the Homestore website, you can see the Addendums tab. Click on it. Look for the PCR or Property Condition Report. It will usually tell you if there are any major issues.

---

[11] Hud homes are sold on the Hud Homestore website, but they also sometimes give the homes to real estate agencies to sell, and they in turn put them out there in the general population of houses on generic real estate websites.

3) Your third option, if you can't arrange an inspection, is to ask your real estate agent to tour the house and send you video footage from their cell phone. This is the least desired option, but if you have a rock star for an agent, it may be possible.

A Screenshot of a HUD Home's Addendums

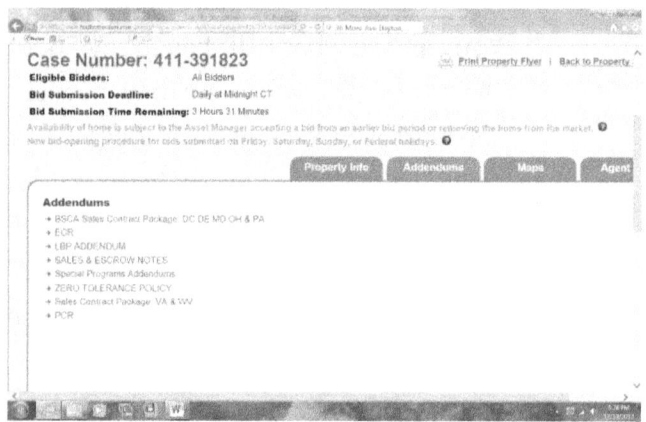

Look for the Property Condition Report

Major Headaches or Good Fortune!

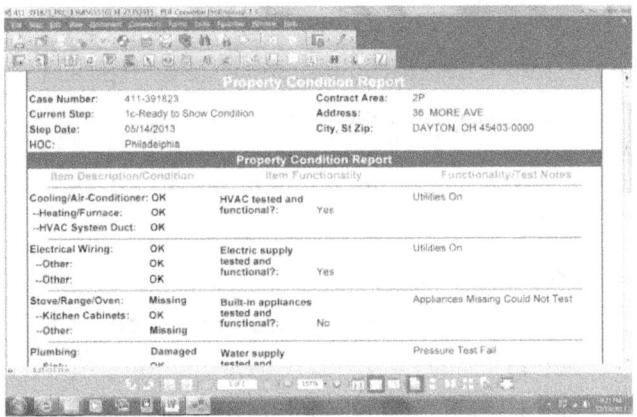

Paying the Bill

If you buy a HUD Home with an FHA loan or other type of mortgage you will have to fulfil the requirements as laid out by your lending agency. Most people who go this route are what is known as HUD as an "Owner/Occupant." You're going to live there.

This book can help in the process of getting a HUD home in general, of course, but the focus is more on investors, so I will not go into buying HUD homes with FHA loans or bank loans.

I am assuming you have a few thousand dollars to spend or even a few tens of thousands, and you want to invest in real estate without too much hassle or expense. This is also my objective.

So basically, you need to make sure that you have the cash on hand to buy a HUD home, because you're going to have to wire it pretty quickly. The earnest money deposit even usually needs to be overnighted. You'll need a cashier's check for that too. I'll go into this whole process in the next chapter.

The Step-by-Step Process

Now it's time to turn our attention to actually making a deal happen. The previous chapters were important, I believe, for helping to lay the mental and mechanical groundwork for a successful HUD deal. But if you're anything like me, you can't wait to get to the "How-to" part.

So here goes. I will walk you through from start to finish how I buy a HUD home. As you follow the steps below, please keep in mind that there are better men and women than I who do this for a living.

There are gurus and masters and people who eat HUD homes for lunch. I'm just a regular guy – a school teacher – who wanted to achieve financial stability through real estate, and who has been making that process happen for just about three years now. I plan to buy, rehab and rent out 2-3 HUD homes per year on the side, and this is what I've been doing and I believe it's going very well. So here goes:

Step 1

I decided on an area that I want to invest in. I know this particular area (Southeastern Michigan) and I return there every year for vacation.

Step 2

I spent some time on Trulia and Zillow getting to know the general home prices and rental markets.

Step 3

I made contact with a real estate agent who is both registered to bid on HUD and also who specializes in the same area as I wish to invest in. I went around with him looking at houses one summer and we got to know each other and I became much more educated about houses and house buying in general.

Step 4

I created an account as a "Public" person at the HUD Homestore website. You cannot register as a "Bidder" unless you are a registered real estate agent who has an account with HUD. Your real estate agent will be the one who submits bids for you.

www.hudhomestore.com

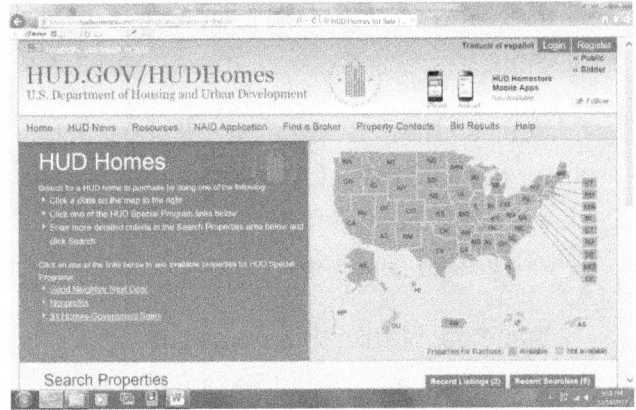

Step 5

Now it was time to browse the Homestore for homes I was interested in and that fit my budget. Go to the "Search Properties" area. Make sure to select "Investor" as your "buyer type." Select the state, and if you desire, the county. For the price range, put in what you like. Right now, I personally look for homes under $10,000. Any other parameters are your choice. [12]

Step 6

The list of homes came up, and for every one I saw that was interesting, I "saved" it by clicking the "save" button on the right of each listing.

You can "Map it" right away if you want, and when I do that, it is to weed out houses that are too far in to major urban centers where ghetto conditions may exist.

Some people like those types of investments (guaranteed Section 8 income), but I'm not so adventurous.

---

[12] Some states have more HUD foreclosures than others. Some cities are bursting with them, while others seem barren. You may not find what you want, where you want it. In that case, you can keep checking back, or you may want to focus on an other area of the state or nation.

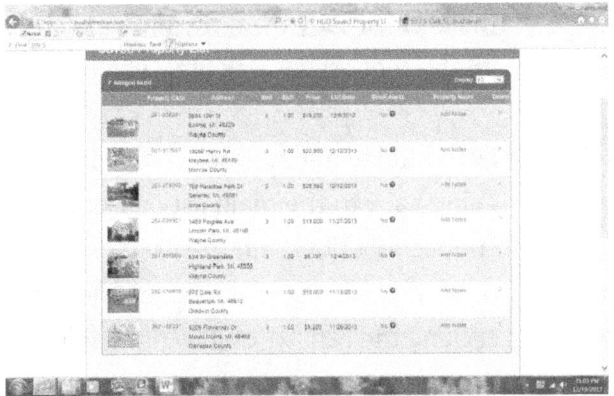

Step 7

After I've perused the many pages of listings (and there will be more pages the higher your dollar threshold is set at), then it's time to look over the ones I saved. If you're still logged into the Hud Homestore, you can either click on "Saved Searches" or the "Public Functions" link right under your name at the top right of the website.

I am going to examine these properties more closely using the following procedure:

A) I will click on each property, one at a time, and map it and look more closely at the location. If it is in a 'bad area' that I know about (since I learned about the area already from my time playing on the real estate websites!)

I will then eliminate that choice by going back to the main list (clicking "public functions" on the upper righthand corner of the page) and then clicking the red "x" on the right side to delete that house from my list. If the property is not in the heart of the 'bad area' but maybe on the edge of town, I usually save it for further study.

B) I will look at the Addendums tab to see if there is a Property Condition Report (PCR). I will use that information, coupled with any photos of the property that are in the listing to get a general idea about the condition.

C) I will look up the address on Trulia and Zillow and see what the deal is. With the neighborhood market. I will be sure to check the prices of the surrounding area on both sites, as well as checking the "crimes" tab on the Trulia listing.

D) I will consult City-data.com for the factors that are important to me.

E) If I am still interested, I will see if there is a listing for this property with an original agent. Both Trulia and Zillow will give the name if one exists. Perhaps there will be more photos or information on their website.

F) I will check hudhomevalue.com to see if there is any bid history.

G) I will use Google ""Street View" if available, to take a virtual 'tour' of the neighborhood.

Step 8

If any listings make it through my process of elimination, then I check my finances to see if I can come up with the money should I win the one of my choice.

Step 9

Now I think of a bid amount. HUD set up their website to compare bids with pre-selected algorithms. Of course, the highest bid will win, but you certainly do NOT have to bid the suggested bid amount in the listing. In general, as long as you're not in a bidding war with a lot of other people for the same house, you can safely bid about 20% less than the suggested bid price.

You could get lucky in two different ways: either the house has sat for a while with no bids and they accept a bid that is even 30%-50% under their suggestion, or someone bid higher than you and you had the 'fallback' bid and thus win. [13]

Step 10

So if I'm ready to go on this deal, I email (or call) my real estate agent. I politely tell him which house I would like him to bid on. I give

---

[13] This happened to me on a $30,000 house once. I was the second bidder and on a whim I bid $3,000. The higher bidder, who won with $7,000 backed out or something. So the next highest bidder was – me!

him the Case Number, the address and the original bid amount. [14]

Then I tell him what I want my bid to be. (Usually 20% less than suggested on the listing.) The agent replies that he submitted the bid, and then I wait.

Step 11

If I win the bid, the real estate agent emails me the good news. If I don't win, well, he doesn't need to tell me! You know that someone won the bid because within about two days the listing will be disabled on the HUD Homestore. Now HUD accepts bids for a property until 12am each day, and if the bid meets the criteria of the algorithm's parameters, then you (or someone else) won!

Step 12

Here's where the hustle happens. If the house you won is being sold directly off the HUD site, you need to have your earnest

---

[14] This information is found on the actual home listing on the Hud Homestore website.

money [15] and a signed contract in the HUD office in just a few days.

Basically, your real estate agent logs in (as a Bidder) and prints out the HUD contract. He shoots it over to you as a .pdf and you have to sign it (IN BLUE PEN) and send it overnight with the earnest money cashier's check by a set deadline that may be only 24-48 hours later.   Please don't overnight things with the U.S. Post Office. The items may arrive too late in the day to be processed. Send things UPS or FedEx overnight and set an early delivery time.

If the house is being handled by an asset management company (HUD does farm out a lot of houses like this) then there is not as much time pressure because the asset manager sets the time schedule according to their own office's functioning speed, but it is still boom, boom, boom. In my case, I overnighted the documents and check to my own real estate agent, who personally hand-

---

[15] Earnest money is a cashier's check, usually for $500 that you have to send right away to show you are serious about the deal.

delivered the documents to the asset management office where they needed to be.

Step 13

So now your contract and earnest money were received (either at the HUD office or by your real estate agent, who then forwarded it or takes it to the asset management agency) and now you wait for the closing. It is usually about ten days after you initially submitted the contract. So how do you close if you are not physically there? Simple: give your real estate agent the Power of Attorney to sign for you.

It sounds scary to give someone else the power to sign legal documents on your behalf, but the POA document will be written in such a way as to ensure that the agent ONLY has the power to sign for you on THIS PARTICULAR DEAL and for nothing else. Don't worry about them ordering your feeding tubes removed decades from now!

The parameters of the POA will be spelled out clearly and in fine legalese. Any good real estate agency knows how to write one of these. Your agent will send you the document (usually as a .pdf that you can print out and examine).

Read it over carefully. Get it notarized, and overnight it back asap. Now there's nothing left for you to do but wire the money when instructed. Your agent can sign any necessary documents to make the house yours.

If you want and can arrange for an inspection of the house, do it now. Perhaps your real estate agent can help, but you will still have to pay for it. You can still back out of the deal if you want, though you might lose the earnest money.

Step 14

When your agent has the closing arranged, he will receive a copy of the final contract with all the final numbers. This will include the final purchase price, the commissions and the closing costs. What? Did you say commissions? Do we have to pay that?

Most likely no. HUD often pays the commissions to both the real estate agents (theirs and yours). That's a pretty sweet deal all around. Now you know why real estate agents are willing to help you buy your little HUD houses. They get paid well for only a few hours worth of work with you.

Your agent, as a courtesy, will email or overnight a copy of the contract to you, so you can see the final deal and make sure everything is okay.

You will see the closing costs and taxes, and be prepared – seeing the large figure you have to pay in taxes will give you a serious Republican Moment as you fume at the high local tax rates. The tax man always gets his. It's not terrible, but for example on my last deal I paid $5400 for a house in a city and had to pay $1600 in closing costs.

The agent will also email you wiring instructions for the money. Go to the bank and wire the money to the account number that is designated asap. Don't try to wire at home from your bank's website. It either won't work or you won't do it right and the whole deal may fall through. Let a bank professional do it for you.

Step 15

If the deal goes as planned, the house is yours after closing. Your real estate agent will get you copies of the closing documents, and as soon as the title is ready, you'll get that too. Now it's time for rehabbing!

If you didn't get an inspection before, now you would do it. If this is a long distance property, you may want to get a property manager. They can be found on the internet in every city and state. If your real estate agent offers this service, so much the better.

From here the subject matter of rehab and rent or rehab and flip is beyond the scope of what I've tried to do here. There's plenty of good books about that. Suffice it to say, a property manager is key to either goal.

This entire 15 step process is the exact same method I have followed to buy many foreclosed properties. Not everyone's experience will be the same. A lot depends on the skill of the agent(s) handling your bids and on how much homework you did on the house and the area.

Suffice it to say, and I think you will agree, this process is not hard at all. You're not wholesaling houses to strangers. You're not cold calling people or building websites or doing any of the other things the masters want you to do.

It's a relatively simple and straightforward process you can use over and over, as you get financially able. With each house, you fix and flip or fix and rent you have more money/cash flow to set yourself up for the next deal, and then the next and the next.

My personal goal is to have around 20 houses, all producing income, in the next ten years or so. (As of this writing I am about to close on my sixth property – woo hoo!) Whatever your own goal, this HUD buying goldmine can be your way to achieve your goals too.

In the next mini chapter, I will highlight a recent deal I did so that you can see the possibilities for you, as well. I'm no genius, but I can do this, and therefore I believe so can anyone – including you! Good luck and good hunting!

Case Study

Flint, MI

I found this home listed on the HUD Homestore for $7,000 in December of 2013. I researched it on Trulia, Zillow and also checked out the city-data.com info. A Google street view tour revealed a quiet, mixed race neighborhood of older folks and families.

What I also found by looking at the maps was that this house was on the periphery of the city. Flint is often known as a very dangerous place, but like all cities there are still nice areas and low-crime, residential neighborhoods.

I know this because I am familiar with southeastern Michigan in general and have been to Flint before (hence my insider knowledge). You too will want to become familiar with an area so you can envision the lay of the land in your deliberations. That will empower you as an investor.

This particular home is near an area with moderate levels of crime, but the house was several blocks away from the hives of 'scum and villainy' as you might say, and it was located on a quiet street.

I also found the original realtor's website and there were ten pictures of the house inside, which was much better than the HUD website which only had four. The rooms, as far as I could tell, just needed paint and some carpets swapped out. Even the kitchen looked like it was a paint job away from success. It was in almost move-in condition! Comparable house prices revealed that the average, similar sized-home in the immediate area was worth $25-$40 thousand dollars.

Wow! I thought to myself. If I can get it for about $6k I would have a great deal. But I was short of cash, so I emailed my real estate agent and threw out a figure of $3,200 for the bid.

He dutifully submitted it, and I certainly did not expect to win at all with such a low ball bid. I also forgot about it because I was busy with another closing at the time.

Lo and behold, the agent emailed me a few days later to tell me that we won the house. I was stunned and elated. Then I checked Hudhomevalue.com to see what happened, and this is what I found.

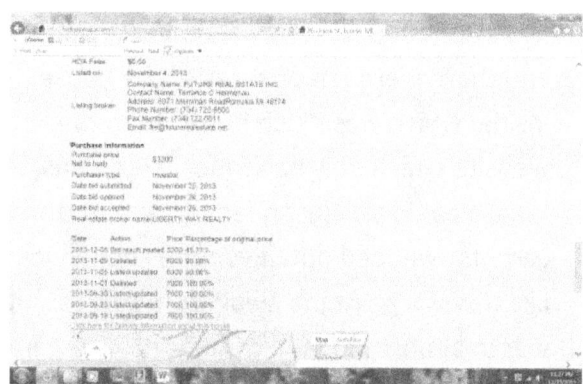

Someone else had won the bid at 7k, but apparently the deal fell through. (If you get your contract in late, HUD drops the deal just like that!) Then someone else won at $6300, but that fell through too. What luck! So my bid of $3200 was next and accepted. Amazing.

My agent emailed me the contract and the POA form. I got the POA signed and notarized. I signed the Contract in blue ink and then overnighted the package back to him with a cashier's check for $500. Then I waited for instructions on wiring the rest of the money, and about two weeks later, I had another house.

I really felt at that moment that this HUD house business was the opportunity of a lifetime for people who want to break into real estate but don't have lots of spare cash lying around.

I had to rehab the house, of course, but my estimate is that it wouldn't need but $3-5k or so to get it rent ready. I have a property manager who runs it, and I get a rent check every month. Even if it's not huge (only $300 after expenses), magnify this by a dozen houses and you have income replacement.

Sure it may take a year to get one up and running, but each year you do it, it gets easier, and as time passes perhaps you're soon doing two a year, or three or more. If I can do this sort of thing, anyone can.

I do hope this book gave you some ideas that are useful for your life, and I pray that whatever your goals are, that you achieve them. I would also like to thank you for taking the time to read how I started in this business, and I hope to achieve my goals even as I hope you achieve yours!

Real estate is the best investment out there, because no more land is being created, and there's always more people. Resolve to learn about this unique way to acquire real estate on the cheap, and take a chance on a property. With proper planning and effort, you can certainly do this. Yes, you can.

Resources for Further Study

Internet Sites

www.realtor.com

www.zillow.com

www.trulia.com

www.hudhomevalue.com

www.city-data.com

www.hudhomestore.com

www.apartments.com

www.realtytrac.com

www.homesearch.com

Books

Forever Cash, Jack Bosch

Rich Dad, Poor Dad, Robert Kiyosaki

HUD Homes Half Off!, Larry H. Goins

Flip: How to Find, Fix and Sell Houses for Profit, Larry Villini

The Book on Flipping Houses, J. Scott

The Book on Estimating Rehab Costs, J. Scott

Fixing and Flipping Real Estate, Marty Boardman

Videos and Shows

Flip this House - A&E

Flip Men – Spike TV

Fix and Flip/Rent Today!

www.ingramcontent.com/pod-product-compliance
Lightning Source LLC
Chambersburg PA
CBHW071756170526
45167CB00003B/1047